THE MATHERS

WEIGHED IN THE

BALANCES

BY DELANO A GODDARD M A

AND FOUND NOT WANTING

BOSTON: Office of the Daily Advertiser
LONDON: Office of Henry Stevens 4 Trafalgar Square
April 1870

To

M L D

Cotton Mather and Salem Witchcraft. By William Frederick Poole. [North American Review, April, 1869] Boston, 1869; 8vo, 63 pp.

Salem Witchcraft and Cotton Mather. A Reply. By Charles W. Upham. [Historical Magazine, October, 1869] Morrisania, 1869; 4to, 93 pp.

Under this Stone lies Richard Mather
Who had a son greater than his father
And eke a grandson greater than either

The Mathers

T IS THE OLD, OLD STORY OF heroes lifted a great deal too high in one century, only to be dragged down a great deal too low in another. For a hundred years after their death the fame of the Mathers, father and son, rode on the crest of the waves. The last blast through Mr Dawson's trumpet has come near sending it into the trough of the sea. Will it ever find plain sailing and fair weather again?

If it were possible to believe that the iniquity of motive and of conduct charged upon these two ministers were truly a part of their character; if it were possible to regard them as the foremost among the guilty wretches at whose door the blame for the dark deeds of 1692 must forever lie, there would still be mysteries in their lives more confounding than witchcraft, and problems in the history of their times which could not be solved. But grant that they were what they professed to be; grant that they were what they seemed to be to the generation in which they lived, and to every generation which followed till the new canon of criticism was laid down in 1831, and there is difficulty no longer. Make just allowance for the exaggerations with which friends and enemies regarded them in their lives, and while the recollection of their lives was fresh in all our New England households, and we have no fear that they will suffer from the ingenious assaults of these latter days.

Contrast with these assaults the testimony of those who knew them, and who saw their light go out. The funeral honors paid to the shade of Hector were tame and weak compared with those of the Massachusetts Province in remembrance of the elder Mather. A mourning multitude that could not be numbered followed him to the grave. The ordinary language of eulogy was too weak to express the veneration and love everywhere felt for the patriarch of the clergy and the friend of the people. "And they buried "him in the city of David, among the kings, be-"cause he had done good in Israel, both towards "God and towards his own house." The son died five years later. Equal if not greater sorrow followed him to his rest.

"Last Tuesday morning," says the New England Weekly Journal of the 19th February, 1728, "died here the very Reverend COTTON MATHER, Doctor in Divinity of Glasco, and Fellow of the Royal Society in London, Senior Pastor of the old North Church in Boston, and an overseer of Harvard College, by whose death persons of all ranks are in concern and sorrow. He was perhaps the principal ornament of his country, the greatest scholar that was perhaps ever bred in it. But besides his universal learning, his exalted piety, and extensive charity, his entertaining wit, and singular goodness of temper recommended him to all that were judges of real and distinguished merit. After having spent above forty-seven years in the faithful and unwearied discharge of a lively, zealous, and awakening ministry, and in incessant endeavors to do good and spread abroad the glory of Christ, he finished his course with a divine confidence and joy the day after his birthday which completed his sixty-fifth year, being born on February 12, 1662-3." On the Monday following his remains were honorably interred, "his reverend colleague in deep mourning, with the brothers of the church, walking in a body before the corpse. The first six ministers of the Boston Lecture supported the pall. Several gentlemen of the bereaved flock took turns to bear the coffin, after which followed first the bereaved relatives in mourning, then His Honor the Lieutenant-Governor, the Honorable His Majesty's Council, the House of Representatives, and then a large train of ministers, justices, merchants, scholars, and other principal inhabitants, both men and women. The streets were crowded with people, and the windows filled with sorrowful spectators all the way to the Burying-place where the corpse was deposited in a tomb belonging to the worthy family."

The pulpit did not spare its praise of the departed. "To see them no more," said the Rev. Thomas Prince, a learned and useful man, "is no "more to see their grave and smiling countenance; "no more to see their gracious and reviving looks; "no more to see their decent and comely carriage; "no more to hear their lively and pleasant voices, "their flaming sermons, their learned, pious, "most instructive and entertaining converse; no "more to hear or to see them in their pulpits, to "meet them in our streets, or to receive them in "our houses; in fine, no more to have their earn-"est prayers, their ready help, their wise advices, "their great and quickening influence in these "degenerate times. But to lose them all, and to "lose them forever! O inexpressible loss! O in-"supportable bereavement!" So Dr Benjamin Colman, who had been tried as only the saints can be tried, by the peculiarities in Cotton Mather, which at this late day have been dug out of their almost forgotten graves for his condemnation, signalized his death by a sermon on the "Holy Walk and Glorious Translation of Blessed "Enoch." "We mourn," he said fervently, "the "decease from us—not his ascension to God—of "the first minister in the town, the first in age, in "gifts and in grace, as all his brethren readily own. "I might add, the first in the whole province and "provinces of New England for universal litera-"ture and extensive services; yea, it may be, "among all the fathers in these churches from "the beginning of the country to this day, of "whom many have done worthily and greatly; "yet none of them amassed together so vast a "treasure of learning and made so much use of "it to a variety of pious intentions as this our "reverend Brother and Father, Dr Cotton "Mather."

Was this all a sham? Were these ministers of the truth deceived? Was this man, of all others, who had lived in a blaze of light from his cradle, and at whose grave friends and enemies alike gathered to cover it with their kind but too generous offerings; who had been forced into the very centre of affairs while yet a child, who was never known to have a secret, and could not have kept it if he had,—was he the designing, plotting, self-seeking, insatiate hypocrite, which it has become the fashion to represent him? Are we to believe that he went about the Province triumphing amidst the assaults of evil angels, glorying in judicial murders, applauding and encouraging them even under the fatal shadow of the gallows, inventing cases of witchcraft when the excitement lagged, and using his learning and his ministry to serve this diabolical passion?

Let us not be misunderstood. The actors in this witchcraft business are not to be judged by any ideal standard. Dr. Colman and Thomas Prince, and the editor of the New England Weekly Journal must stand aside. So also must Robert Calef,—whose writings are not contemporaneous with Salem Witchcraft,—when his testimony comes in conflict with the texture and spirit of the lives of those whom he has accused. If the Mathers cannot stand by their own merits they must fall. The guilt and the folly of that period they share with the great and the wise of their time. But if any trust can be put in human testimony, the charge of deliberately getting up and ingeniously prolonging that bloody and fearful crusade against the supposed powers of darkness, cannot be maintained against either of them. The charge as it has taken shape in Mr Upham's last contribution to the literature of witchcraft, and as it now stands, is as follows:—

"By stimulating the Clergy over the whole country, to collect and circulate all sorts of marvellous and supposed preternatural occurrences, by giving this direction to the preaching and literature of the times, these two active, zealous, able and learned divines, Increase and Cotton Mather, considering the influence they naturally were able to exercise, are, *particularly the latter*, justly chargeable with, and may be said to have brought about, the extraordinary outbreaks of credulous fanaticism, exhibited in the cases of the Goodwin family and of the 'afflicted children' at Salem village." [Historical Magazine, October, 1869, p. 131.]

The substance of the charge appears again and again in the course of Mr Upham's ingenious work, sometimes qualified and explained as above, sometimes without qualification and with indignant feeling. Let us see how it applies to the elder Mather. The affliction of the Goodwin children began in 1688. The cases of Margaret Jones of Charlestown, of Mary Johnson at Hartford, of Goodwife Knapp at Fairfield, of Ann Hibbins in Boston, of Katherine Harrison at Wethersfield, and many others, were long before familiar to the minds of the ignorant as well as of the intelligent. These trials and executions occurred in the provinces of New England before Increase Mather had written a line on the subject of witchcraft, and while Cotton

Mather was in his cradle, and before he was born. Meanwhile the witch stories then current in English literature and the writings of learned men who gave countenance to them, were in the hands of hundreds of New England families, before the writings of the Mathers were known beyond the little circle to whose wants they ministered.

During the period just preceding the Goodwin affliction, the attention of the elder Mather had been much occupied with the disturbed affairs of this Province. Early in that year he went to England to lay the wrongs of his people before their sovereign. He remained abroad upwards of four years, engaged with the engrossing cares of his mission. Up to that time the subject of witchcraft had not specially interested him. If he had spoken of it or preached upon it, it was doubtless with the thoroughness and earnestness to be looked for in one who stood as a watch tower among his people, and suffered nothing which affected their happiness or welfare to escape his notice. The chronology of his published works shows very little bearing directly or remotely on the subject to that date. Of the thirty volumes he had printed, one only, and that incidentally, treated of the mystery of witchcraft. When he returned from England with the new Governor in 1692, the fanaticism of that year was at its height. The local ministers and justices in Salem had done their utmost, and filled the prisons with accused persons, now awaiting trial. If there had been evidence that Increase Mather had anything to do with producing this particular outbreak, we think that Mr Upham would have found it and used it. He has found nothing of the kind, and it is useless for any one else to make the search. We find in his "Reply" no such imputation, unless the interest expressed by Mr Mather at the assembly of ministers in 1681,—eleven years before,—can be so used against him; and his interest here consisted in an exhortation to the ministers to preserve a record of important facts as materials for history.

The new Governor, finding prompt action imperative, as it seemed, took counsel of the chief people and officers of the Province, and appointed a special court to conduct the trials, selecting for this purpose the deputy governor, and for the rest "persons of the best prudence and "figure that could then be pitched upon." There were no educated lawyers in that court—there were none in Massachusetts. But the members of the court were familiar with affairs, and with the practice of the English courts in like cases. The Special Court has been pronounced by recognized authorities as technically illegal; but the judges acted in accordance with their authority as they understood it. They lost prestige through their conduct at these trials, but not the public confidence; for Stoughton, Sewall, Winthrop and others continued to exercise high civil and judicial functions in the Province during their lives. They were familiar with the writings and decisions of Sir Matthew Hale and other eminent jurists, and with the opinions of wise and learned men who had made a study of witchcraft for a century before. They appealed for their justification to the authority of these men, as well as to the more commanding authority which came to them with the voice of inspiration—"Thou shalt not suffer a witch to live."

The trials went on apace, the gallows was glutted with the number of its victims. Under the pressure of the prevailing panic, no one could stop them. Increase Mather took the opportunity to write a book. That was the resource and entertainment of the Mathers in all weathers. But this book—Cases of Conscience Concerning Witchcraft—was of unusual significance. It was written to allay excitement, to refute false evidence, to awake the slumbering reason, to inspire caution for the future. It vindicates not only its author, but the much maligned ministers of Boston, from the imputations under which the later histories have placed them.

Mr Upham especially has done injustice to this book. He does not mention it in his History; he misjudges it in his "Reply." In the last he says, "As I had no particular interest in determining "what his views were,—as a careful study of the "tract, particularly taken in connection with his "*Postscript*, fails to bring any reader to a clear "conception of them; and its whole matter was "altogether immaterial to my subject,—I did not "think it worth while to encumber my pages with "it." But to one seeking for the truth it seems to be the very thing with which his pages should have been encumbered. Increase Mather stands charged, page after page, with giving a certain evil direction to the preaching and literature of the times. The Cases of Conscience Concerning Witchcraft,—perhaps the most notable of all his contributions on this subject,—shows that Mr Mather's influence at that critical moment was not in the direction which Mr Upham alleges, but in the opposite direction. The study of that tract is essential to a clear understanding of the conduct of the ministers at that time, and as such it cannot be left out of the case with fairness, or with a proper regard for truth. Mr Upham confesses that he does not understand this book. He does not approach it with an understanding spirit. It is inconsistent with the theory to which everything else appears to be sacrificed.

But where was Cotton Mather all this time? Mr Upham holds him "particularly" chargeable with these occurrences, and the later historians with here and there an intelligent and just exception join in the indictment. He was then a young minister in the twenty-sixth year of his age, and in the third year of his settled ministry. He had published at that time a few books, and a goodly number of tracts, but nothing on the subject of witchcraft. He did not take that up seriously till the phenomena happened at his own door, and the community around him was groping for some faint light to guide its steps. Believing in the reality of witchcraft with all his capacity for belief, he was zealous among those who entered into the warfare against it. In this belief he was in the company of Sir Francis Bacon, and Sir Thomas Browne, and Sir Matthew Hale, and of philosophers and jurists and statesmen without number on whose fair fame their connection with witchcraft has left no enduring blemish. That Cotton Mather has fared so much worse than these, in the estimation of those who accept the current histories of the events he took part in, so much worse even than the judges who conducted the trials and the citizens who sustained them to the last, may be traced to the fact that his personal importance at that time has been very much overrated, and his real connection with the witchcraft trials has been grievously misunderstood.

He had been much talked about, and overpraised on account of his birth, his reputed learning, and the hopes which the religious sentiment of the time reposed in him. He greatly over-estimated himself; but the same diaries to which he entrusted his most secret thoughts, and which have been ransacked for evidence to condemn him, show how earnestly in his hours of fasting and vigil he sought deliverance from the proud thoughts which fly-blowed his best performances, and from the affectation of preëminence far above what could belong to his age or worth, and above others who were more deserving than himself. He had many ways of doing good, but in his view the first and most effectual agency was prayer. He appears among the Goodwin children three months after their afflictions began, but in the company of other ministers called together for counsel and prayer. He took one of the children to his house and endured its strange performances for several months, in the hope of testing again the efficacy of prayer. He visited the wild Irish Glover woman in prison, and her soul went to its last judgment upon the wings of his prayer. Whatever judgment may be formed of him from single extravagant sentences detached from his account of the Goodwin matter, there is nothing in his conduct then, literally nothing, which is unbecoming to his character for thoughtful, sympathetic and gracious piety.

We come now to the trials at Salem—passing over much, for we can touch but one or two points in this voluminous controversy. We have seen how little warrant there is for the theory that Increase Mather had anything to do with the Salem outbreak. Mr Upham makes much account of the intimate relations between him and the new government under Sir William Phips. Sir William was appointed at his suggestion. Three of the counsellors were of the Mather church. The rest owed their official elevation to the same friendly influence. "It "could not have been otherwise," says Mr Upham, "than that he should have passed under "the control of the Mathers." "The Mathers "were a power behind the throne greater than "the throne itself." Cotton Mather, in his youthful exultation at the course affairs were taking, made a foolish entry of the fact in his diary. He exaggerated his importance in this connection, as his impulses often led him to do; but Mr Upham takes him at his word. The annalists of the time, with the single exception of Robert Calef who disliked the young man, did not so regard him. Governor Hutchinson does not mention him in the account of the Salem delusion. Thomas Brattle, whose stanch disbelief in the methods of the court would have compelled him to speak of Cotton Mather if he had had a tithe of the influence which Mr Upham imputes to him, does not mention him. If he had then passed from the scene he would have been forgotten; or if he were remembered, it would have been as one who played a singular but quite subordinate part. In spite of his great attainments and his precocious advancement, his chief and most enduring title to fame was won subsequently to that brief episode of mystery and terror.

But conceding that the power of the Mathers over the government at this time was so great as to make them morally responsible for its conduct, let us be consistent, and, in the absence of evidence to the contrary, hold them responsible for its conduct when the Governor returned from his fort-building expedition at Pem-a-quid, and bade the headsman pause in his deadly work. Mr Upham takes it for granted that when the Governor returned and found what mischief had been going on in his absence, he decided to break from the influence of the Mathers, and run the government on his own account. The evidence on which he relies to show this break of sympathy was the next election, in which ten anti-new-charter men — Mr Upham calls them "Anti-Mather men"—were elected. This election, however, did not take place till May, 1693, when the executions and trials were ended. The council had consisted of twenty-eight members, all "Mather men." The election of ten old-charter men did not materially alter the political character ot the council: and even Phips was offended at these changes, as appears by his vetoing the election of Elisha Cook, the champion of the new-charter men. There is not a shadow of evidence that any break of sympathy occurred. On the contrary, the way had been prepared for him by the ministers, and he followed in the course they pointed out.

It can be readily believed that the argument of the Cases of Conscience had been used by Increase Mather in his extended intercourse with his friends. Immediately upon its appearance, "the Governor pardoned such as "had been condemned; the accused were in all "cases acquitted; the confessors came, as "it were, out of a dream wherein they "had been fascinated; and the afflicted in most "instances grew easy." Governor Phips was dissatisfied with his associates and rebuked them in his letters to the government at home. "I "have grieved to see," he says, writing in October, "that some who should have done their "Majesties, and the Province, better service, "have so far taken counsel of passion, as to "desire the precipitancy of these matters." Mr Upham, using every thing for his purpose, adds with astonishing presumption, "This refers to, "and amounts to a condemnation of, the advis-"ers who had influenced him to the rash meas-"ures adopted on his arrival." To whom it really referred is made plain by another letter of a few weeks later date, when the Governor found it more necessary than ever to justify himself, in which he said: "Not being versed in law, I "have depended upon the Lieutenant-Governor, "who is appointed Judge of the Courts, to see "that they be exactly agreeable to the laws of "the English nation, and not repugnant in any "part." This was in February, 1693. The advice of the ministers recalling the attention of the court to its obligations in this respect was printed in June, 1692, when the frenzy was at its height.

The ministers were the first who took issue with the court. To sustain Mr Upham's theory of the Mathers, it is necessary to break the force of this important fact. It is necessary to show that the ministers were ignorant of the ordinary meaning of the words they employed, or that their apparently good advice was a trick, under the cover of which they hoped the prosecutions might be more vigorously and more zealously urged forward. Think of it a moment. Here were the ministers of Boston charged with the most solemn duty which could be imposed upon them: the minds of the most sober and prudent men in the province filled with amazement and consternation; those who it was supposed were gifted with some judicial knowledge, and "should have done "their Majesties better service," taking counsel of passion, and registering the edicts of a community which was "beside itself;" here were the abused ministers, trying, with such poor light as they had, to bring the court and the people to reason. They were themselves the neighbors and the personal friends of many of the judges, and they believed that witches who were justly accused should be put to death. But they believed also in the rights of innocence, and resolved to throw around it all the protection in their power. If in their sermons, or their written discourses, they had sometimes spoken with exultation of the visible triumphs of the Great Adversary, it was as some patriots lately spoke of heart-breaking defeats in battle—as the preparatives and forerunners of victory. They were bound to recognize the well-meant efforts of the court to prevent the spread of witchcraft, and to urge the speedy and vigorous prosecution of such as had rendered themselves obnoxious. But language cannot be clearer than that in which they urge and entreat that the method of proceeding in future cases should be changed. They urged the need of a very critical and exquisite caution in these and all like prosecutions; an exceeding tenderness toward those that might be complained of; the exclusion of matters of presumption which were not worthy to be matters of conviction; the exclusion of noise, company, and openness that might too hastily expose them that were examined; consultation with such judicious writers as Perkins and Bernard, whose books were known to the magistrates as against the use of spectral evidence; and first of all and above all, a constant reference to the directions given in the laws of God and the wholesome statutes of the English nation. It was in June, 1692, that the Governor and his council asked advice, and the ministers gave them this. Cotton Mather was one of the youngest of their number. He had a gift for "quick and sud-"den composures," and he put the results of the conference into form as it now stands. The liberal and thoughtful men of the Province were fast coming to this view; but this was nevertheless in advance of them. Take it altogether, in its relations to the prevailing sentiment, as the expression of men who had no motive in life but the service of their fellow-men and the glory of God, as they understood it, this Advice is as honorable a memorial to their fidelity as the wisdom and humanity of that age affords.

It is singular that Mr Upham never printed this Advice of the Boston Ministers of June 15, 1692, until after it appeared in Mr Poole's Vindication of Cotton Mather, in the North American Review of April, 1869. And now, when it has become so prominent a part of the record, Mr Upham is forced, in defence of his theory, to put upon it a construction contrary to the plain and ordinary meaning of its terms; to say that it is in Mather's "characteris-

"tic style" of appearing to say one thing when he was really aiming to enforce another; that it was skilfully and artfully drawn; that a careless reader, or one whose eyes are blinded by a partisan purpose, might not see its real import, and that it was considered by all the judges, and the people in general, as fully endorsing the action of the magistrates, and advising its speedy and vigorous continuance. We find no proof of this; we find nothing to sustain a plausible inference of it in the annals or the traditions of the time. On the contrary, there is abundant concurrent testimony to the truth of Mather's own explanation of this document, written a short time afterward, when, if Mather had spoken falsely, Robert Calef could have gathered a cloud of witnesses to overwhelm him. The manuscript from which we quote, the original of Cotton Mather, has been for many years in the possession of the American Antiquarian Society at Worcester:—

"For my own part," he writes, "I was always Afraid of proceeding to Convict and Condemn any person as a *confederate* with afflicting Demons upon so feeble an evidence as a *Spectral Representation*. Accordingly I ever protested against it, both publicly and privately; and in my Letters to the Judges, I particularly besought them that they would by no means admit it; and when a considerable Assembly of *ministers* gave in their Advice about that matter, I not only concurred with their Advice, but it was I who drew it up."

This advice unhappily was not followed. The court reässembled on the 30th of June and the trials and executions went on. The critical and exquisite caution recommended by the ministers, the judicious counsel of Perkins and Bernard, the wholesome statutes of the English nation, were alike set aside. But the efforts of the ministers, aided by the inevitable reäction against the late appalling excitement, were doing their work among the people. Governor Phips came home from his eastern journey, saw his opportunity, and the trials stopped. Must we apply one rule to the Mathers in May, and a wholly different rule in September? Were they so great in May that they could make and unmake governments, and hold in their mighty leash all powers temporal and spiritual, and before the summer was over were they so weak that neither governor, magistrates, nor people would do them reverence? If the rule of criticism which is now applied to the Mathers were applied to the other great and good men who were contemporary with them; judge them by detached incidents, by detached passages, torn from the context of their thought and life, the best of them could not stand. It would matter little how pure, how honest, how consistent, how humane, how serviceable they were, if they were to be condemned out of the mouths of their enemies, or upon the confession of their own short-comings.

We turn with a sense of profound and grateful relief from this long "Reply" to the friendly and judicious portraits of these men preserved in Dr Robbins's History of the Second Church, where the historian, speaking not as a partisan or a eulogist, represents them in the light in which they were regarded by good men who knew them during the long and useful period of their lives after the witchcraft-season passed away,—recognizing the mixture of good and error there was in them, the good vastly overbalancing the error, their superficial and venial faults overshadowed by inherent and deeply-rooted virtues. "I trust," wrote Dr Robbins in 1851, "that truth is dearer to me than "the reputation of one whom I venerate; and if "the truth required that the image of one of my "predecessors should be taken down from the "shrine, which it has occupied for more than a "hundred years in the church's reverence, and "publicly dishonored, I could bow the head in "silence, though I might not sympathize with "the spoiler, nor be accessory to the deed"

It was not necessary to yield to this humiliation then; and it certainly is not necessary now. Then, as now, there were powerful and honored assailants; but our historian did not appeal in vain to the eternal law that merit shall overmaster the influence of the strong, and disannul the adverse judgment that seemed, and was intended to be, most just. The historical record was clearly and unmistakeably on his side. To the courage and critical discrimination of Mr Poole in our day is due the honor of disentangling the web ingeniously woven anew round these illustrious men, and placing them before the world in their true characters once more. We welcome his elaborate, but still too brief vindication, in our leading Review, which, in spite of Mr Upham's heavy broadside against it, stands, as it seems to us, unshaken in its material statements, the nearest approach we have yet had to the true version of a period and of men that, after all that has been written about them for nearly two centuries, are still so little appreciated and so little UNDERSTOOD

END

www.ingramcontent.com/pod-product-compliance
Lightning Source LLC
LaVergne TN
LVHW011127110826
845150LV00008B/2268

* 9 7 8 1 4 1 8 1 9 5 4 6 5 *